Snow Falling on Snow

Spirituality Books by Robert J. Wicks

Simple Changes (Thomas More)

Everyday Simplicity (Ave Maria Press)

Sharing Wisdom (The Crossroad Publishing Company)

Living a Gentle, Passionate Life (Paulist Press)

After 50: Embracing Your Own Wisdom Years
(Paulist Press)

Circle of Friends (with Robert Hamma) (Ave Maria Press)

Seeds of Sensitivity: Deepening Your Spiritual Life
(Ave Maria Press)

*Touching the Holy: Ordinariness, Self-Esteem and
Friendship* (Ave Maria Press)

Seeking Perspective (Paulist Press)

Living Simply in an Anxious World (Paulist Press)

Availability (The Crossroad Publishing Company)

Self-Ministry Through Self-Understanding
(Loyola University Press)

Snow Falling on Snow

Themes from the Spiritual Landscape
of Robert J. Wicks

Robert J. Wicks

Paulist Press
New York/Mahwah, N.J.

Acknowledgment

The author is grateful to Ave Maria Press for giving him permission to use material from *Touching the Holy* and *Seeds of Sensitivity*, and to Paulist Press for allowing him to extract sections of *Living Simply in an Anxious World*, *After 50*, and *Living a Gentle, Passionate Life*. To enable readers to better enjoy the quotes as meditations, in some cases the material has been slightly adapted, so please refer to the original books if you wish to see the exact quotations.

Jacket design by Cynthia Dunne.
Interior design by Lynn Else.

Library of Congress Cataloging-in-Publicaton Data

Wicks, Robert J.
    Snow falling on snow : themes from the spiritual landscape of
Robert J. Wicks / Robert J. Wicks.
      p. cm.
    Includes bibliographical references.
    ISBN 0-8091-0531-4 (hardcover : alk. paper)
    1. Spiritual life—Christianity. I. Title.

BV4501.3.W53 2001
242—dc21

00-052402

Published by Paulist Press
997 Macarthur Boulevard
Mahwah, New Jersey 07430

www.paulistpress.com

Printed and bound in the United States of America

Contents

Dedication

For Michaele and Peter Kulick,
my wonderful daughter and son-in-law

Snow Falling on Snow

In a cozy little corner
I sit and pray,
wrapped in a warm sweater
with a candle lit
before a mysterious icon.

Outside, the snow is swirling,
the wind whooshing
and the tree branches scratching
against the house,
wanting to come in.

Then, in the spaces in between,
when the wind is forgotten
and all is quiet…
I open my heart
to listen.

And as I hear the peaceful sound
of snow falling on snow,
my soul slowly softens…
and my worries retreat
to the edges of my room.

*Finally I realize with joy
that no matter how uncertain
life may become,
I will always be safe and warm
when I am at home with You.*

Amen.

Snow Falling on Snow

～ A Prologue ～

Kind words often come at the most surprising times.

In the midst of a retreat I was offering for missionaries working in Thailand, Bangladesh, Nepal, and Cambodia, a priest said to me when we were alone: "As I was reading your latest book I faced a dilemma. I wanted to read it faster in order to see what you were going to say next. But I was afraid if I did that, I would miss much of what you had to say to me. Let me tell you. You are easy to read, but you sure pack a lot into a little book!"

I was happy to hear his comments because, as he says, I really try to "pack it in." People are so busy and over-whelmed today. Time is at such a premium that my books are, by design, quite compact. I purposely make an effort to keep my manuscripts brief. Then after my wife, Michaele, edits them, they become even shorter!

Within each of my books there are sections that represent the spiritual and psychological anchors for the work. They are the themes that I hope the reader will especially remember and pray over. In essence these are the points that prompted me to write the book in the first place.

These themes are sometimes reflected back to me by those who discuss their spiritual and psychological journeys with me. Graduate students in my spirituality or counseling courses often quote these key points as they present their own beliefs and ideas. Readers have encouraged me to gather together the themes from my various books so that they would be more readily available for reflection. Finally, I have used this wish as an impetus to develop a new book designed to do just that.

First, I asked Vilasini Balakrishnan, who was very familiar with my work, to carefully cull from my books what she felt were the most essential themes. She then extracted quotes that she found especially relevant and organized them in a way that they could be easily shared with those interested in the integration of psychology and spirituality. I am very grateful for her discerning spiritual eye as well as the many, many hours she dedicated to this project.

I then edited the material Vilasini gave me in order to make what was small even smaller and more appropriate for people's busy lives. The final steps included review by Marie Gipprich, my wife, Michaele, who edits all of my writings (God bless her!), Maria Maggi of Paulist Press (who offered constant encouragement at each phase of this project), and Karyn Felder who typed the final draft; I am grateful to all of these people for their fine efforts and encouragement.

My hope is that these reflections will be used as meditations for a quiet evening at home or an afternoon away from it all. Maybe the reflections could be read one by one in the early morning before going to work or at night before retiring. Possibly this collection could serve as a companion during a day of recollection, a retreat, or in a faith-sharing group. In other words my goal is to provide themes to seed the soul with ideas, hopes, and questions that would encourage a life of greater peace, hope, and holiness.

The themes I am best known for are included in this little book. I have filled the pages with suggestions, reflections, and ideas on perspective, passion, relationship, self-esteem, availability, clarity, ordinariness, and prayer.

I'd like to think that the content represents, as a whole body of work, a spirituality of gentleness, deserving of the choice of the Zen image, *snow falling on snow*. I hope the words contained in these pages, read slowly and quietly, will soften your soul and open you more and more to receive the love and enlightenment of God until your whole spiritual landscape has been altered into something even more beautiful than it is now.

In the back of the book there is a guide to the sources of the quotes. This allows for further reading or rereading, as the case may be, of the books from which the material was excerpted, in the event that you are looking for a more in-depth coverage of a particular area.

Finally, I must say that undertaking this project was a real joy for me. I loved working on it with the people I acknowledged earlier. To share some of my main ideas, feelings, and beliefs about the spiritual life in a brief meditative form was a real treat for me. And, it is in this spirit that I share the following series of reflections with you.

Robert J. Wicks
Loyola College in Maryland

Themes from the Spiritual Landscape of Robert J. Wicks

I

Experiencing the Lord

Prayer
Scripture
Silence and Solitude

Kneeling in Silence

Most of the time I pray and sing
while sitting or standing straight.
But now
the only way to release my soul
is to gently kneel and wait.

Ordinarily a few spoken words
would open up my heart.
But now
to hear Your gentle voice
deep silence needs a place.

My soul is now too lonely
to hear just spoken words.
And sitting or standing
before You
no longer bears my faith.

So I quietly kneel
in reverence
until Your Silence comes
to touch the sadness in my soul
and to heal me...once again.

~ Quiet Space ~

To be involved with God the first thing each day centers us on what is important. It helps us to be awake to the day stretching out before us, one that may be our last. And morning silence and solitude can enable us to better come to our senses and be in the now. This is especially important so we don't miss those interpersonal encounters that might bring us closer to God if we weren't nostalgically reflecting on the past or preoccupied with the future.

But above all, it is the quiet prayerful space of the early morning that enables us to be better attuned to God's particular call for us each day. Without such an intentional space for prayer, hearing the "voice" of God becomes quite difficult. For, as we are constantly reminded by spiritual writers: "There's always music amongst the trees in the garden, but our hearts must be very quiet to hear it."

~ A Few Moments ~

A faithful schedule of a few moments of daily prayer will set the stage for a more mature relationship with God in which more time will be desired and spent in stillness with the Lord.

When we start each day by sitting down with our morning coffee or tea to spend some brief quiet time with the Lord, God's grace will lead us into greater divine union. Moreover, even on the busiest of days, this modest beginning is worthwhile because we cannot so easily shunt aside our time with God with the excuse: "Oh, I'm in too much of a rush; I'll pray later." After all, it is only two minutes, and one of these days there simply will be no later!

~ *Desire and Distance* ~

What keeps us from true prayer?

In a world so filled with greed, anxiety, pressures, money problems, confusion, and conflict, we do very much want the solace and challenge of the truth. We do want to gamble with our lives for the ultimate relationship. We do want to embrace the negative feelings of depression, anxiety, and stress that come into our lives and sit, stand, live, work, and play before God. We do dearly desire the growth-full opportunity to find perspective and unity within our questioning, torn heart and within the world that often tensely surrounds us. We do want our dull, subtly idolatrous world made new.

But the step toward God often seems so hard, so impossible, and foolishly (as is probably our habit) we blame God for this and fail to see our role in our experience of distance and alienation from the Divine.

～ *True Prayer* ～

Pray now, reflect during the day, pray always, and most of all pray *truly*. In other words, don't worry about what you say, how you say it, what you think about, and don't strain yourself. Don't be concerned whether it is perfect or not—just love!

True prayer is always possible. The question that needs to be answered is not whether opening up a dialogue with God is possible. Rather, the question is: Am I in my self-involvement, insecurity, and denial ready to open myself up to the overwhelming generosity and challenges of being in a *real* relationship with God? And in the service of making a personal response possible, am I willing to be aware of the need for:

1. being beautifully "ordinary" in a world so anxiously smitten with the desire to deny death and God and be seemingly extraordinary;

2. being open, truly open, to the wonder and awe that

is in front of us right now and continually surrounds us everywhere;

3. seeking perspective amidst the joys and turmoil of everyday life.

How we are aware of these needs and seek to honestly respond to them may well determine whether true prayer can grow, deepen, and expand within us to the point that when someone asks: "How is your prayer life?" without knowing it they will really be asking: "How is your life?" Although we will have quiet time in solitude to spend in unique friendship with God, the relationship will always be there before us. The awe will not leave us even when our eyes are closed. That is the goal we must embrace; there is no desirable mid-ground.

~ *Honesty* ~

Often the problem is that our prayer is too artificial, bland, and compartmentalized. If our prayer is dull, we must ask ourselves: When was the last time we spoke with God about things that really mattered to us in our daily lives?

Do we share our angers, joys, impulses, secrets, addictions, and anxieties? Do we talk to the Lord about our perversions, desires, needs, resistances, and failures? For instance, when have we last said to God: "I love you," "Down deep, I doubt you exist," or "I hate the way you are running this world!"

Where is the passion?

If God is to be real, if our faith is to be real, then our prayer must be real and include everything. Everything. If we are afraid to speak about such things as our pettiness, embarrassing moments, addictions, and anger, then how can we take the first step toward dealing with them? How can we admit that we are helpless and at present not willing to change? Such honesty is the very essence of a thrilling life of prayer. How can we be sensitive to God and expect God to be sensitive to us if we are artificial in our presentation of who we are?

⌒ *Balance* ⌒

True prayer challenges us to be ruthless in our sensitivity to the truth in honest interactions with others, as well as in our intimate interaction with God in silence and solitude. To forget our time alone with God is to court the disaster of undisciplined activism. But to ignore the holiness of our time with others is to set the stage for quietism.

A dedication to balancing quiet reflection, involvement, and action will help us accept the contradictions and mystery of living out a street spirituality in today's world. It will help us to be sensitive enough to uncover a blueprint for living, loving, and working. This is especially needed in a world that seems so lost, so intent on steeling itself against our self-awareness and sharing of gifts and burdens of life with one another—at a time when healing interactions are most needed. Such a commitment to prayer and action in the midst of so much confusion and darkness today will lead us to experience the promise Jesus made to us so many, many years ago: "I shall not leave you orphaned; I shall come to you" (Jn 14:18). And, what more can we ask of the Lord than that?

~ *Surrender* ~

Contemplation is first and foremost a gift. It involves the freedom of God as well as our own initiatives. Consequently, one of the first questions we need to ask ourselves in prayer concerns the attitude with which we are entering the relationship. If it is with the respect, humility, and awe that are part of love of the Divine, then we are coming to the encounter with a proper sense of the depth involved. Too often, we fear risking the presence of the Spirit in our lives in a way that ends in our not being able to control God's presence or message. We say we want the love of the relationship, but often we finish the sentence under our breath with, "in our way and on our terms."

Once again, there is no bargaining with freedom. Either the relationship is real and open, or it isn't. And if it isn't, then prayer suffers accordingly.

⁓ God's Will ⁓

For years I would read the scriptures and quietly pray that I could be more obedient to God, more single-hearted. For years I would pray that I could be enthusiastic rather than exhibitionistic, achievement oriented rather than competitive. For years, being an impetuous person, I prayed that I would not be swayed by people's reactions—positive or negative—or be a victim of my insecurities and need to be liked, but only be concerned with doing God's will. And for years the sense I received in prayer was simply: "Just do my will; it is enough." To this I would always reply in a very down-to-earth way: "It's easy for you to say! I just can't do it. It's not enough for me. I need a reward. If it's not people's good thoughts, if it's not the applause, if it's not my image, then I must have something."

Then one day, when I was praying for something else, I sensed a response not only to this request, but also, finally, to my original one as well. The impression I had was this:

"You have asked that you not be concerned with your image or success but only with my will; your prayer will be answered now." To this I became anxious and was even sorry I had prayed for help at all. I was concerned that with the gift more would be asked of me. Yet, this insecurity did not dispel the sense I had of God's presence. And the impression I had of the Lord's response continued clearly in the following manner: "If you seek to do my will and focus only on it and not on your success or the way people respond, you will find you won't have to worry about whether or not you are accepted and loved by others. You shall have another reward that will make you secure—in *every* lecture, in *every* therapy hour, in *every* encounter on the street, when you concern yourself only with doing my will and forget about the reactions or results, you will be in the *Presence of the Spirit*…Is that enough?"

⌐ *Simple Steps* ⌐

Liken yourself to a beautiful original part of creation—a true work of art. Then each day ask yourself how you are living: either in ways that show gratitude for this beauty or in ways that indicate how you are defacing it.

Read a little scripture each week to see what God has said to others like you who are searching for the Truth. In this way you may learn from the past in order to know better which way to step in the future.

Continue to do some simple things for others in need and look for God's presence as you do these little good works.

And finally, take quiet time each morning to reflect on your relationship with God.

∼ *Prayer: The Uncharted Zone* ∼

Prayer has gotten a bad name. It is often labeled as nice, warm, lovely, sweet, and soothing. These descriptions—and maybe even some other more accurate, positively oriented ones (i.e., "peaceful")—are somewhat misleading. For while the prayer life will surely bring with it at times a deep sense of well-being, this experience is neither the goal nor necessarily the immediate result of a deep daily dialogue with God. Since any good intimate relationship is a precarious adventure at best, a committed relationship with God, guided by the process of prayer, is truly a dangerous as well as remarkable journey *if it is really undertaken in the spirit of the First Commandment.* If we were honest with ourselves about our relationship with God, I think we could all write a book entitled *God Is Solidly Number TWO in My Life!* We frequently put so many things and people (especially ourselves) in front of God.

Therefore, we are rarely aware of the danger, the depth, the challenge, and the core of a real relationship with the Divine. We muse about it so much of the time rather than deciding to leave our world of rumination and procrastination and enter into a clear covenant with the Lord.

⁓ *God's Rhythm* ⁓

Once when I was speaking with my spiritual director about prayer, he recognized that while I was valuing the importance of having my work be a prayerful experience, I was also missing an important element.

He said: "Well, of course you are right to see prayer in the broad context of things and appreciate your work and leisure as forms of worship. However, some caution might be important here. You see, when you receive the grace to pray during the day, there may be a temptation during this period to go and do something else. You may make a phone call and it may be a good thing that you are doing. You may go read a book and that may be beneficial as well. However, when you are done with these actions, the grace to pray, meet, and get to know God in silence and solitude may be temporarily gone as well. So, be attuned to the graces you are given for different things, including prayer, and try—in God's rhythm—to respond accordingly."

"Distractions" in Prayer

There are times when certain distractions to prayer repeat themselves and seem to demand center stage. A friend might be sick, we may have financial problems, there may be an issue we have with alcohol abuse, there may be someone who frightens us or with whom we are angry, or we may have sexual feelings that bother us. In these instances, many people experienced in spiritual direction suggest to us that we shouldn't try to go around or ignore these interruptions, but see them as aspects of life that need to be integrated in the Lord. So, instead of fighting them, we present them to the Lord for healing attention. In laying them to rest in the Lord, we can then concentrate on God instead of ourselves and our problems.

Stay Put

To deal with resistance when we enter prayer, the first commitment must be to "just" stay put, not run away, and be disciplined and regular in our attention to our time with God. When we are faithful we may initially feel somewhat lost and "between things." This is good in a way. It is like stretching to wake up—wake up in this case to the fact that we don't feel like we have God in our lives. The alternative to accepting the fact that we are all beginners at prayer is worse. For without quiet time in the morning or evening to slowly make our trust in God more visible, we tend to drift between guilt and impulse. And "drifting" is far different from "flowing." Drifting has no purpose, no divine theme; flowing with life is prayerfully being free and at home in the present, no matter what happens. Even when spiritual darkness and boredom occur during these periods, with prayer they lose their threat, become somewhat irrelevant, and (more important) are eventually passing experiences if only we stay with our prayer.

~ *Where Is the Passion?* ~

Love is the basic prescription for prayer that is ill and limping.

Without love there is little passion in our sensitivity to God's presence in our life. And without fire in prayer, there is little motivation to continue. The result is periods when prayer is dull or absent. The question we must ask about our prayer is: "Where is the passion?" These periods we spend alone thinking about God may be nice but they lack the drama and intensity of true prayer.

Without fire there is no real prayer. The difference between a prayer life with real fire, light, and warmth, and one in which we talk or think about fire but act in ways which show that true passion is missing is that in the latter the heart of a real relationship with God is also absent. The question again is: "Where is the passion?" Or, put another way: "Where is the fire?"

⌒ *Impasse* ⌒

There are times when all of the careful problem solving in the world will achieve nothing. We are at an impasse. This is a time of special appreciation of our dependence on God's mercy and guidance. It is a time for prayer, true prayer. It is also a time for patience, trust in the Lord, and a sense of alertness to the new ways God may be calling us to find *the* Way in a darkness we can't control, remove, or analyze. The simple spiritual reality is that God will provide the light, in the way and at the time that God's providence, not a human time frame, determines. We are free, but we often forget that God is too.

If we wait and don't run, we will see what we need to see. If we stay and don't try to distract or numb ourselves, we will hear what we must hear. And if we hold onto our hope and don't drown ourselves under rumination over the ruined expectations, if we open ourselves when our grieving for what we have lost is done, then we will experience what we really need. We will be given what we can receive now, so we may become deeper persons on our journey.

~ *Nurtured by the Word* ~

Henri Nouwen offered me simple words of advice many years ago that are still valuable today—for me and I believe for everyone:

> Take a few moments every morning in silence and solitude. Read a few passages from Scripture. If you have a daily book of biblical readings or a lectionary, use that. Then once you have read these words from Scripture, sit quietly and let them nurture you in silence. Do this every day without fail and you shall be all right.

~ *Relaxing with Scripture* ~

Sacred scriptures need to be at the heart of our reading regimen. Once again, amount of time is not as relevant as regularity and the quality of attention we give to God's words to us.

Reading sacred scriptures for five or ten minutes each week may not seem like much, but how many of us do it? How many of us relax with scripture so we can be with God in a way that we can be taught, encouraged, challenged, and given a sense of peace?

~ *A Simple Regimen* ~

When we encounter sacred scripture with sensitivity and a sense of energy, the persons in the stories become friends with whom we can almost converse, and themes from the Bible become places for us to test our identity and reflect on our way of living. This results in a change in our prayer and life.

A good indicator of this is when scripture mentally bubbles up to the surface of the rough seas of our daily problems to help us gain perspective and have courage. Prayer doesn't replace scripture; it is a new page in it. Therefore, a simple regimen of reading scripture for its own sake—not as part of a religious service, for study, or homily preparation—is essential. Sensitivity to God includes, first and foremost, a radical sensitivity to the word God has given us in sacred scripture.

～ Lectio Divina ～

Read sacred scripture each day as usual, but at least part of the time do it in the spirit of the practice of *lectio divina*. By that I mean we should first select a few minutes each day to read the scriptures prayerfully and with a sense of expectation and surprise. Then, while reading the passages, do a spiritual exegesis, that is, read the words with love and a sense of discovery until something seems to strike home. Finally, sit with that passage as one would with a good friend—not thinking or analyzing, but instead remaining in a quiet, listening spirit, so the word can nurture and challenge you.

～ *A Passionate Reading* ～

Sacred scripture is the story of God and of God's relationship with people. Unfortunately, these words are often treated like dusty old furniture instead of the living, proven antique vessels of truth that can free us from the chains of contemporary secular thinking.

When we read scripture with a real sense of passion, the words of wonder in it can inspire us during our different moods:

- when we are depressed, they support us;

- when we are filled with joy, the words can dance with us;

- when we are bored, they can challenge us anew to see how we have set aside God and life behind a veil of secularism, ingratitude, and entitlement.

Just reading the Bible for itself and not as duty is a nourishment that can't be rivaled.

Be Courageous... ~ *Stop Avoiding God* ~

What we can do is to stop avoiding the opportunities to truly read the scriptures, to sit in silence, and to patiently and courageously face our emotions so we can learn about ourselves and our movements toward and away from God. If we are patient, if we are open, we will learn—we will feel the presence of God.

~ *The Window* ~

Confucius said many, many years ago: "Look at this window: it is nothing but a hole in the wall, but because of it the whole room is full of light. Being full of light it becomes an influence by which others are secretly transformed." This window of which he speaks is, for me, silence—the true silence that allows God to speak.

~ *Approaching God* ~

Silence and solitude are necessary if we are to hear God's voice. Just as necessary is our willingness to be faithful by giving the Lord the time for quiet prayer each day.

How we pray is, of course, up to us. Each of us must take off our shoes and meet God on holy ground in our own way. However, the following basic ideas, which most of us learned formally or informally at some time or other early in our religious training, are worth repeating here: (1) Find a quiet place to sit and relax. (2) Put yourself in the presence of a loving God and wrap yourself in gratitude. If you don't have these feelings, pray for them as you continue. (3) Either take a centering word (such as *Jesus*) or read a few passages from the Bible or a spiritual book. (4) Sit with the spirit of what you have read or quietly repeat the centering word over and over again. If you become aware of anything else or are distracted, just let the issue move through your mind and out. If it persists, then hand it over to God rather than preoccupying yourself with it, which, after all, serves no purpose. (5) Sit quietly like this with the Lord in love for ten or twenty minutes a day on a regular basis, and your relationship with God will grow.

～ *Two Minutes* ～

Periods of *silence and solitude* during the day are essential. When asked for the most basic suggestion I can give about prayer, I always say the same thing: "Take two minutes out each morning in silence and solitude, wrapped in gratitude before the Lord."

If more time is desired and taken, fine. But a *minimum* of two minutes each day is essential to center oneself, know who one is, and move into the day with a sense of true identity.

The whole process is very simple. Find a quiet spot in the house. If your house is crowded, stay in bed a bit longer or use the time during your morning shower. In this space center yourself on God by using a word (*Abba, Love, Friend, God, Mother...*), a line from scripture, or by first reading a few words from a book on spirituality.

Then, image yourself being covered with the clear, comforting Light of God and simply remain quiet for a few minutes in the presence of God. That's it. Nothing to achieve. Nothing to do. Just be with the Lord before the day gets going.

～ *Letting the Fog Lift* ～

Why don't we spend more time in silence and solitude and give the loneliness we often experience a chance to blossom? In this way, the negative feelings and hidden denials deep within can rise and perch in front of us so we can address them with a God who loves us.

Why do we continually fail to see that the chance for real joy is wrapped in unexamined anger, apathy, and confusion? Why do we frequently miss the fact that our peace is shrouded in a fog of anxiety and preoccupation? When will we realize that if we stay with these feelings and worries, they will clear, and amidst the pain and joy of life we will find Truth, we will find God?

~ *Silent Awe* ~

The wonder and awe of the world we and others fabricate is paltry compared to God's offerings. We need only look at the colors of nature in the fall or the fury of a storm in the winter to see what God can communicate to us even when we can only "half-see" through the distractions of being preoccupied with the hurts of the past and a desire to control the future, while the vibrant present before us remains almost totally ignored and unappreciated.

This is why silence and a sense of presence to the now are encouraged by so many spiritual writers. Silence breaks down our walls, and attention to the now helps one to see what has long been hidden behind them.

~ *Silence and Solitude* ~

By wrapping ourselves in silence, solitude, and gratitude, we can open our hearts in contemplation again and again to perspective and simplicity. We can hear God in a world of sorrows, joys, uncertainties, and limits because the lost art of listening, really listening to the universe, can be gracefully recovered again and again in the Sabbath experience of silence and solitude.

~ *Our Desert* ~

When we sit prayerfully in silence and solitude, we are entering the desert, our desert. In this sacred space, the goal is not to hide from others, devoid of pain, or to hold ourselves apart from and above the community in which we live. It is to receive the grace to learn to face ourselves directly so we can learn to live ordinariness, to live ethically and generously with others.

The Garden

I want to walk in the Garden
and have You as a companion,
as my grandfather did before me.

So You can softly encourage
and help me avoid the stones
that trip me when I'm alone.
I need to hear the birds sing
together with Your voice
in the shade of the old trees.

And see Your smile
as the sun touches the flowers
and makes their faces laugh.

Yes, I can't walk alone in the garden.
I need You at my side
just as my grandfather did before me.

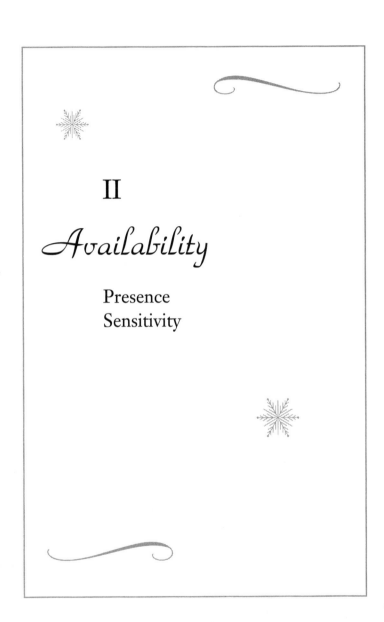

II

Availability

Presence
Sensitivity

The Circle

Lord, there is so much pain
in the world.
Where do I begin to help?

"*Start in your circle.*"

But when I help
my family and friends
often they really don't appreciate me.

"*But I do.*"

And when I reach out
to my coworkers
some suspect my motives.

"*I know what is in your heart.*"

Still, I think I should do more
to help those I don't know
who are suffering in the world.

"*Then, widen your circle.*"

But by myself I can't
do much to lighten
their great darkness.

"Yes, I know. That is why I am with you."

If only I could believe
You are with me.
If only I could really see you, Lord.

"Open your heart
in prayer
and you will believe and see."

What will I see, Lord?

"That as you walk
through the day
I am the center of your circle."

~ The "Circle of Grace" ~

The development of our own inner life and our reaching out to others are intertwined. They make up a circle that surrounds and feeds both our own spiritual selves and those with whom we interact during our lifetime. If this "circle of grace" is broken and spirituality is divided from compassion, two dangerous extremes may result.

One is that spirituality may develop into a narrow form of piety called quietism. We will withdraw from the world and, instead of finding time with God, we will simply be alone with our own ego. Security and comfort will become our obsession, and the perspective that can be brought to us by our interaction with others will be lost. We need compassion for others to help center us and to bring out the love that is within us so that it doesn't wilt or lie dormant. On the other hand, when we seek to be compassionate without time for prayer and quiet reflection, our reaching out runs the risk of degenerating into compulsive forms of giving that may be lavish but not very genuine.

The circle of grace is simultaneously the basis and fruit of a gentle, passionate life. It feeds single-heartedness and challenges it. It helps us to keep perspective so that we don't inordinately pull back from life or in some way forsake taking care of ourselves to wind up burned out and discouraged. Therefore, to keep the circle intact, we must attend to both quiet reflection on the one hand and active sharing with others on the other, so that our life remains balanced, alive, and filled with fresh energy, wisdom, and *self-respect*—an important aspect of the journey toward a gentle, compassionate life.

⌒ *The Gift of Presence* ⌒

"Presence" is truly one of the best gifts we can offer to others in need. The value of presence to another person should not be understated. When we sit with people in the darkness and "help them cry" we model hope and new possibilities in ways even we sometimes don't realize.

⌒ *Being With* ⌒

I don't think that any of us fully realizes that being listened to is so very, very important. More and more, I have learned that attentively *being* with someone is essential for the person's health and growth. In order to develop, we need to be heard by others, to share our life story as well as our feelings, ideas, fears, and hopes. That is why speaking with a friend or family member in the evening about the little activities of our day is so healing—even if we do it over the phone or by writing a note.

~ *Listening* ~

One of the reasons listening is a rare gift today is that so many of us (possibly because of our anxiety) strive too hard to do something useful or to be immediately helpful in some tangible way. The problem is that in the process of doing this we fail to really listen to a person's pain. In becoming stressed out ourselves over what we need to do to be "successful" with someone in need, we often fail to realize the pure value that is listening, in and of itself. Furthermore, when we're not observing the situation for what it really is, we not only miss a chance for understanding, but occasionally may even make the situation worse by acting too impulsively.

~ *Look* ~

Caring is not saying a lot of words to people, not completing a compulsive list of works, and not trying to respond to everyone's expectations (including our own!), but trying, with all of our being, to develop an attitude of openness and alertness in our interactions with others, which is based on only one thing: the desire to look for and bring God *everywhere*. And a cornerstone of such a wonderful form of caring is the beautiful gift of *presence*.

~ *Faithfulness* ~

When people seek our caring presence, in addition to listening and an openness to new perspectives, faithfulness is also crucial. But although we may know and accept this, faithfulness to people who are in pain, depressed, under stress, or experiencing a great loss is never easy. This is so even when we feel pretty certain that God is calling us to be with that person.

Our faithfulness cannot rely on the gratefulness, compliance, or results we see in or receive from others. If we feel that we need people to be thankful, then surely our efforts won't last long. Faithfulness instead must rely on our deep belief that the very act of caring is worthwhile. This is hope in action.

Faithfulness, then, is modeling ourselves after the Lord, who has been and remains worthy of our trust. Faithfulness is a way of saying to the world that I believe in God's goodness no matter what sadness or cruelty I see. Just as it is a beautiful gift to us in our own covenant with God, faithfulness is also one of the greatest gifts we can give to others.

~ *"Unlearning"* ~

If we are to be successful, we must know the right kind of effort to make—an effort that includes embracing a radically new attitude and living out of a more honest identity. One way this can be accomplished more easily is through a deep appreciation of the process of unlearning, so that relearning and responding in new creative ways can really become possible.

All through the history of the human race we have heard stories of people being asked to let go, unlearn, reform, renew, and accept an identity that is more in line with who they could become rather than who they have settled for being because of the presence of anxiety or ignorance.

Like them and others throughout history, we are now called to unlearn much of what we have absorbed that is untrue about ourselves and others so we can have an attitude of sensitivity. This will allow us to be open to new realities and new possibilities and to find our own true name and identity. We can then model this for others so they can also be empowered to see and take their places of dignity in the world.

⌒ *Openness to Others* ⌒

When we view the lives of people, both in history and from our own families or neighborhoods, who have responded sensitively to the emotional, spiritual, social, and physical needs of others, we see that they often possess inner peace and joy. Unlike those of us who narrow our vision or merely give compulsively to those in need, such persons have found ways to risk sensitivity, no matter how harsh the times. In turn their attitude and actions demonstrate that they can see how this attentiveness to others is connected with increased self-awareness and a deep sensitivity to God in prayer.

⌒ *Spiritual Sensitivity* ⌒

A deep sensitivity to God is the source of all sensitivity. With an awareness of God in our lives, we are able to embrace two essential truths: we are not alone, and we must be sensitive to the needs of others. With God in our lives we feel integrated, centered, hopeful, loved. Without the presence of the Lord, we feel unloved, alone, and so burdened by the presence of human cruelty (including our own if we are honest) that we tend to become judgmental, passive, cynical, and periodically given to despair. At times like these, sensitivity to ourselves and others doesn't really seem very possible.

Life is very difficult and harsh at times. A person who lives a truly prayerful life—a "street spirituality"—knows this and doesn't avoid such painful realities. Instead, he or she brings them to God during liturgy or community prayer, quiet periods of solitude, and in reflective moments of prayerfulness during the activity of the day.

～ *Accepting Failure* ～

The attempt to live a sensitive life brings with it a certain amount of failure, and the aspect of this failure that hurts the most is the recognition of the personal limits, poor motivations, and personal inadequacies we have hidden from ourselves. The problem with intimacy with people in pain is that while we try to help them trust and open themselves to their inadequacies and faults, we are called to see the blemishes that sit right alongside our gifts.

~ *With God in the Darkness* ~

Rather than giving in to the natural tendencies to avoid the darkness that we experience in our own hearts and the world at large, facing it is of great value in these times. While we may not be able to prevent life's storm from chilling our soul, we must do what we can. And if it is being done in the correct spirit, it will join us with others seeking to do the right thing and, of ultimate importance, it will join us with the living God, who is the source of real peace, our peace. Once again, a deep sensitivity to God is at the source of a sensitivity to ourselves and others—even when, maybe especially when, there seems to be so much darkness present.

~ *Resurrection Road* ~

If we remain sensitive to the presence of God in faith and in prayer, even in the darkness of confusion and suffering, the darkness will teach us; it will become the light. And with a new, graced sense of simplicity, we will have the ability to be sensitive to this different light and recognize it for what it truly is: the love of God present to us at a time when we are most in need of a spiritual companion to help us on our road to Emmaus. It is a road with necessary crosses but, just as certainly, a road to real resurrection.

~ *Self-Knowledge* ~

The darkness of a true encounter with self can be like a psychological mirror, crisply reflecting those partially hidden and disguised parts of our personality that keep us chained to a spirituality which isn't open or mature enough. It reflects our own rigid defenses, personal immaturities, unresolved repressed issues, hidden motivations, tenacious defenses, erroneous (yet comfortable) self-definitions, and our chameleon-like behaviors. In essence, it confronts us with the darkness of our unintegrated self.

What then does this experience of darkness call us to do? I think it calls us to take steps to live life differently. It invites us to shape a life where we can approach both God and ourselves with a greater sensitivity. We can face both our darkness and our joy with a healthier sense of self and a more responsible, honest style of relating.

I would like to outline four areas of focus where I think it might be particularly helpful for us to take steps toward honest sensitivity with self, God, and others. We need to cultivate:

- a willingness to review basic ways in which we can be more responsible psychologically in how we live in general;

- a method to uncover our own spiritual theology;

- a process for reflecting theologically each day on how we are living;

- a practical method for discerning God's call to us in life and an awareness of how we can best be involved in this process.

~ *Theological Reflection* ~

It is important to take time out each day to experience God more intimately in our lives. Certainly we do this through regular prayer and a periodic taking stock of our spiritual theology. But we also must deepen our awareness of the reality of God by trying to see *how* God is present and active in our lives, a process generally referred to as theological reflection.

The elements of theological reflection vary somewhat. They also depend upon the tradition of the spiritual guide with whom we might consult or the authors we regularly read on this topic. However, many would agree that the process includes at least the following actions in some form:

1. Determine the most important concrete occurrence during the day.

2. Image yourself being back in the event and recall it in as much detail as possible while reflecting on how you were feeling, thinking, and behaving at the time.

3. Establish why this particular event had such a personally felt impact.

4. Relate it to scripture as best as you can. Think about the New Testament and ask: "What would Jesus have done in these circumstances?" Or, "What do I believe Jesus would say to me now if he were here?"

5. Establish what you feel you can learn from it on a deep spiritual level (and, if possible, write it down in a copybook you save to journal in the evening).

6. Put the newfound insights gained from reflection into action with a specific plan for the future.

So, a good reflection that brings God into our lives includes: recalling concrete events that had an impact (either positive or negative); the use of imagery; a simple application of scripture; and a willingness to learn from the interaction in a way that will lead to action.

Appreciating Ourselves and Recognizing Our Foibles

An important way to strengthen our ability to be sensitive is to readily appreciate ourselves and recognize our own foibles to the point where we can gently laugh at ourselves. When people enjoy themselves and can get in touch with their own beauty, they can even reach the point of teasing themselves. This is a wonderful illustration of the sensitivity people can have about themselves, which then frees them to be more open to others instead of being overly protective due to unnecessary problems with public self-image or self-esteem. As a result, when this happens we can enjoy their own recognition of their foibles through the sense of humor they display about them.

Sensitivity and a sense of humor go well together. They set the stage for us to relax enough to see ourselves honestly, not take ourselves too seriously, and to learn how we can best be a sensitive healing presence to others without unduly carrying the burden of our pride. The joy of being at ease with oneself is a great and gentle gift; without it, sensitivity to others becomes just another chore rather than a wonder to experience even in the darkest of times.

Risk, an Essential Piece of Love

An attitude of love and sensitivity sounds pretty, but in the concrete it takes a good deal of work and a willingness to risk. Yet willingness to risk is the most essential attitude that those of us wishing to experience a spiritually vibrant life must assume. Without a willingness to risk involvement in real relationships, loneliness, apathy, and an unhealthy preoccupation with self are all that remain.

The Trap

So often we worry about ourselves and our own sense of security. We actually forget that the best way to be a self-confident and faithful friend of God is to be more sensitive to the needs of others, rather than to be overly concerned with ourselves. We need an appreciation of the wonder of giving, the deathlike quality of greed, and the neurotic concern many of us have with being taken advantage of by those to whom we give something. Otherwise, we will be trapped in the moody, emotional prison of overpreoccupation with self.

~ *The Paradox* ~

As we listen to others in a world that seems to no longer want to listen, we begin not only to hear the voices of others but also to become more sensitive to our own inner voices as well. We recognize the paradox that we can't truly know our own story in any rich detail until we are willing to listen closely as others tell theirs.

~ *Total Sensitivity* ~

If today we wish to respond to the gospel call to empower others in a way in which we can experience the peace of God as well, we need a threefold commitment to sensitivity: a *total* sensitivity to self, others, and God. This must certainly include a willingness to be aware of others in ways that go beyond the usual limits of our so-called openness. But this, in turn, must also be based on a ruthlessly honest appreciation of who we are now and who we might become with a bit more courage, humility, and prayer.

This is sensitivity in its totality. This is, I think, an example of true spirituality. And this is, I believe, what we are called to do and be in today's harsh world.

Let Me Remember

O gentle and caring God. . .

When I feel frustrated by someone's ingratitude and seemingly impossible expectations,

> *let me remember his neediness or fear of saying "Thanks."*

When I face a person's rage,

> *let me remember the pain she has long endured at the hands of many others so I can give her the space to share her anger freely and without fear.*

When someone sees the world (and me) in extreme negative and positive ways,

> *let me remember that I am neither the devil…nor, for that matter, am I God.*

When people are very troubled and I begin to feel overwhelmed by it all too,

> *let me remember that "simply listening" is truly a quiet, great grace in itself.*

And, when I see a person making the same mistakes over and over again,
>let me remember *that sometimes I'm not such a winner myself!*

Yes, as I sit with others who are sad, in pain, under stress, depressed, anxious, and afraid,
>let me remember *your gentle faithfulness,*
>*So I can be present to others in the same way you always are to me.*

Amen.

III

Clarity

Perspective
Awareness
Identity

Softening the Soul

Lighting a candle
in a dark room
is a small gentle act of peace.

When the match touches the wick
time slows down
and the race to the future ceases.

Worries are consumed
anxiety burns out
and I sigh…deeply.

Watching the flickering light
is a graceful prayer
which eases my stress and lessens my strain.

Finally when the flame goes out
I turn quietly back
to the events of the day

and find everything changed because of the time
I sat softening my soul
…by candlelight.

∽ The Proper Attitude ∽

We need a way of viewing ourselves and the world that truly allows us to appreciate all the wonder that is in and around us and keeps us from being overwhelmed by the negative in life. Memorizing techniques is not what changes us; rather, it is in having *the right attitude*—one that will offer us the angle of vision that we need to respond to pain and negativity.

Zen experts put it this way: Face reality and unwilled change will take place. Jesus put it another way: "Do not worry about how you are to speak or what you are to say; for what you are to say will be given to you at that time" (Mt 10:19). In other words, to use yet another scriptural metaphor: "If your eye is healthy, your whole body will be full of light" (Mt 6:22). Perspective as an outgrowth of a healthy psychological and spiritual attitude is truly what matters! When we view ourselves, others, and the world properly, then all we look at finds its proper place.

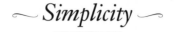

Simplicity

Encountering simplicity in life is wonderful, for with it comes a true sense of what's important. When we are simple people, we are sensitive to ourselves and our lives in such a way that we tend to see things in their proper perspective. In turn, with perspective our life—even during pain and confusion—has a sense of simplicity and direction that never totally disappears, although it may be partially hidden from us at the time. It is something delicate yet strong, which doesn't depend on our emotional state or the impact of others.

A Different Vantage Point

Perspective allows us to ask new questions of life. It enables us to look from the vantage point of being on a high mountaintop, so that we can see sunsets and horizons spiritually and psychologically in such a way that our life changes and we can behave differently and live more peacefully and simply.

Perspective can allow little children in poor countries to play kick-the-can and laugh as they watch the rusted piece of tin jump from competitor to competitor. Simultaneously, a lack of perspective and gratitude may cause a rich tourist to complain if the bus is five minutes late. Instead of taking those moments of quiet to be at peace and filled with gratitude, the impatient tourist becomes so aggravated that he misses what is there to enjoy now in his life. The choices as to whether we live life joyfully and with appreciation are, in many cases, indeed up to us.

～ *Perspective* ～

Perspective reveals what is before our eyes, including what we haven't been able to see because we didn't have the "vision" to experience what was there.

Perspective also helps us to see the strengths with which we have failed to credit ourselves. Too often, we are able to see our problems much more clearly than our talents, and that's a shame.

No matter what happens in our lives, it is very hard to maintain perspective and see what is *really* important in life. Perspective, a sense of gratitude for the people and gifts in our lives, and respect for the limits of life as well as the inevitability of death (*our* death as well as the deaths of our loved ones) need to be sought each and every day.

~ *Prayerful Perspective* ~

Prayerful perspective can come out of meeting our emotions with honesty, interest, and a desire to learn. In our quiet moments of reflection, we can sense the pulse of our feelings, but this is not enough. What we feel must lead us to what we think and believe about ourselves, our Lord, and our universe. It must also lead us back again and again to the sacred scriptures and must call us to our knees again and again to realize the place of grace.

~ *Goodness Surrounds Us* ~

Every effort needs to be taken to become more aware of the positive in our environment, whether it is something impersonal (weather, food) or relational (a compliment). In doing this, the whisper of praise and the presence of goodness in our environment can be received more readily on a daily basis. The strength and balance that such an awareness will provide will be amazing.

Encounters with God

Be as open as possible to being surprised by encounters with others. We must not look for our God in reactions that we feel would be important and right. We must position ourselves instead to see whatever we will see amidst the joy, pain, apathy, anxiety, peace, depression, or tension we experience. When we are truly open, we will be surprised by something in the encounter. And that surprise—that unique presence of God—can be called by another name: *holiness*.

The Beauty Already There

Seeing reality with a sense of awe is based on the willingness to embrace a new perspective. Therefore, we must do all we can to seed such an attitude marked by gratitude—a deep gratitude that tells us even our daily life is a gift, a gift that we can easily ignore while we fantasize with desire about what is not in our lives. The shame of it is that when we are involved in this type of yearning and fantasizing, we miss so much that is in front of us and wind up feeling even more needy. The saying, "To whom much is given, more will be added," is certainly apropos in this instance.

Feeling guilty or helpless about our inability to be grateful for what and who we are serves no good purpose unless it wakes us up to the fact that we have a need for understanding the beauty that is already in our lives. Maybe we miss so much because no one educates us on how to fill our emptiness with awe and goodness. Maybe we just don't understand how to learn and teach one another how to "take in" all that is *already* in our schedule, environment, and life. Maybe we need to learn how to see in a new way. Certainly such a course in perception would be well worth the effort.

~ *Passion for Inner Truth* ~

A spirit of openness helps us to realize that we are always bound at some level and that we need to be intrigued and innervated by the mystery of this resistance rather than discouraged by it. We need to see our resistance clearly so that truth and self-knowledge can help us "move our heads" rather than keep them where the rocks can fall on them. In other words, we need to examine our own resistance to profitable change.

The first step in doing this is to embrace the passion of truth as we look at behaviors that seem to be holding us back. When we are honest with ourselves in reflection, pray with a real desire to be naked before God, and try to be as honest and vulnerable as possible with a mentor, counselor, or spiritual guide, then the seeds of change and a melting of our resistance can become possible in mysterious ways.

~ *A Small Price* ~

We resist looking at our sins and failings because we believe they prove that we are people who should not be appreciated and loved.

In prayer, when we challenge our shame before a loving God, our sins come to light and we recognize that we are not the same as our sins. We see again the difference between guilt that results from admitting I've *done* something wrong and shame that is produced by the pervading erroneous belief that I *am* someone wrong.

To break through the chains of shame so we can take our place in the world, the hidden elements of sin must come to the surface, be faced, and shared with a loving God who tells us, "Go and sin no more" (Jn 8:11). I guess the old saying is valid: "The truth will set you free…but first it will make you miserable." However, this temporary misery is a small price to pay for the freedom that comes with realizing that we are known and loved by God.

~ *Street Spirituality* ~

A deep sensitivity to God—a street spirituality—is a call for us to live in the classic tension of welcoming God into our lives, both in our transformative private and communal prayer and during those times of encounter with others during the activity of our day. To avoid one or the other side of this tension is to court either the disaster of quietism (a prayer life that is unreal and indulgent) or undisciplined activism, which, eventually, will only lead to withdrawal and discouragement. A deep sensitivity to God is the source of our sensitivity to ourselves and others.

Although solitude and praying in silence form a part of following Jesus' example, we must also include sensitive intimacy with others. Time alone with God is not meant to replace the communal sense of God that is experienced when two or more are gathered in the Lord's name. We recognize that our quiet reflection must be tempered and needs to be fired by interactions in which we are open, vulnerable, and looking for God beyond our projections and needs. Street spirituality, then, is the place where contemplation and action meet.

~ *Attitude* ~

While our behavior in the service of God is essential, it is the underlying attitude that determines how and with what intensity we will begin and continue our work. If we are willing to learn about ourselves as well as others, the work will continue. If we truly and tenaciously love ourselves as God loves us, the work will continue. If we are not seeking positive responses and great results but are trying to focus on finding God, the work will continue. But if our motivations are poor and our behavior lacks love (of *both* ourselves and those we serve), then the work will dry up and the seeds of despair, confusion, and bitterness may find root.

Principles of ~ *Self-Respect and Clarity* ~

When I have made a mistake or feel anxious, I need to separate what I have done from who I am.

When I feel badly about myself as a person, I must see if I am embracing an irrational belief about myself. I need to take a distressful feeling as an opportunity to uncover a style of thinking and believing that undermines my self-respect or desire to understand and correct my behavior.

I must be sensitive to irrational thoughts and be willing to challenge and dispute them. Thus I can affirm my self-respect and model it for those whom I wish to help. A common example of this is the irrational belief: "I must be perfect or successful all of the time." This is ridiculous and impossible. It is based on such irrational beliefs as: If I make a mistake, it undoes all that I've accomplished; it is all my fault; it means I am a terrible, unspiritual person; it will completely destroy my reputation in everyone's eyes; it cannot lead to anything good.

Since I am the one person with whom I will have an intimate relationship for my entire life, I need to take care of myself at least as well as I would care for others. Therefore, when I am feeling poorly about myself, I need to take steps to unconditionally accept myself and to help myself gain clarity and perspective in the same way as I would for someone else coming to me for empathy and support.

~ *Our Own Goodness* ~

Having a good relationship with ourselves is essential to overcoming resistance to change or seeing the truth about ourselves. In counseling, the foundation for helping people make progress is the relationship between the counselor and the client. If he or she has a high degree of trust in the helper, the person seeking assistance is more willing to take a risk than if there were little confidence in the person offering guidance.

Once again, the same is true with respect to our relationship with ourselves. It is often easier to trust others than ourselves, so we need to work even harder on self-appreciation. When we trust in our own goodness and value and are able to articulate clearly the gifts that we have been given in which others take joy, then we will be more apt to risk change and to see the truth about ourselves, even if it may seem negative at the time.

That is why fostering self-esteem is so important. When we have sound self-confidence, we can toughen our psychological skins to criticisms from others as well as to self-criticism, so that we can admit our foibles, tease ourselves about them, learn from them, and keep going.

～ Seeing with the Eyes of God ～

Unlearning requires a ruthless willingness to be open to the truth about ourselves and brings with it great rewards in self-knowledge and freedom from being bound up in our defenses or shadow. It also loosens up creative energy to experience ourselves, others, and God in new ways.

However, to be involved in unlearning relies heavily on our ability to be very clear that we are loved and special in the eyes of God. Without this, our self-awareness will slowly turn into self-condemnation and will be a doorway to guilt and shame rather than to knowledge and growth.

"Place" of Refuge

One of the most compassionate things we can actually do for others is to develop greater self-esteem ourselves.

People who know themselves and are at peace always have something to share—no matter how difficult the situation turns out to be. They are alive, and those who encounter them enjoy the possibility of living with more clarity and meaning in their lives because of the gentle space they offer. People who are in touch with their own gifts, who are grateful to God for them, and who seek to nurture these talents in themselves are like oases for the worried, poor, depressed, and oppressed of the world. They are a "place" of true refuge.

— Building Self-Respect —

Enhancing one's self-respect is much more than an exercise in gaining greater personal comfort and security by improving one's image. It is nothing less than a psychological responsibility and a spiritual battle to accept the challenge to have greater sensitivity to the grandeur we have inherited, to be a living example for others who expect us to guide them, and to recognize that self-respect is a unique form of grateful worship to a God who has singled us out to be a reflection of divinity.

Self-respect is more than an ideal to wistfully think about. It is something to pray for faithfully each day and to act upon by reviewing the negative thoughts we may have about ourselves. There are many ways for us to inadvertently devalue ourselves as persons, whether because of something we may have done, as a result of what people may be saying negatively about us, or because of some physical, psychological, intellectual, economic, or other lack, real or imagined. When we vigorously oppose such thinking we are showing active respect for ourselves as creations of God.

~ *The Freedom to "Be"* ~

The call to be everyone but ourselves is so loud that we are usually not able to hear the "little voice of God" calling to us, to everything and everyone in nature to be fully themselves. I find it hard to believe that human beings have the undesirable distinction in nature of being the only ones running away from the reality that has been given to them. Nothing else in nature does this. Isn't it ironic that, given the scale of plants, animals, and humans, we are the only species that spends so much time trying to be something or someone else? Tulips seek to be what they are—tulips. Dogs and bears simply respond to the call of nature to be fully what they were created to be. Then there are we humans; what are we doing? We're trying to look and act in ways that would—to our eyes—make us more attractive. We are trying in so many ways to deny what realistically makes us—to our minds—ugly.

Consequently, in our prayers, in our sitting down and wrapping ourselves in gratitude for all we are and all we have been given, one of the first preparations needed for true prayer to take place is: to be who we are before God.

~ Jesus' Example ~

Due to our lack of complete trust in God's revelation that we are made in the divine image and likeness, most of us get caught up in trying to be extra-ordinary. We become insecure and are tempted to rest our sense of self on something less than God's love for us. As a result, we waste our energy worrying about whether we are liked, respected, effective, or as good as other people.

We certainly can learn from Jesus' example in this regard. In contrast to our concern with what other people think of us, Jesus did not compare himself to others. We cannot find a single instance in the New Testament where he clung to his divinity. He wasn't obsessed with his image, as we so often are with ours. Instead, he was only concerned with: (1) trying to be who he was called to be (obedience); (2) being in solidarity with others (community); (3) doing everything in the right Spirit (love). This is only possible for us when we, like Jesus, (1) feel deeply loved by God; (2) see the essential value and challenge of "simply" being ourselves; (3) resist the temptation to create a false image of ourselves. Both our anxieties and the values of our society can seduce us into trying to develop, or hold onto, another image of self—even if it be a seemingly desirable or good one.

~ *Our Word* ~

We waste so much energy in being people we feel we should be, others want us to be, or we would like to be, rather than who we are being called to be by God. That is why it is essential to begin the search now for the identity we have been given by God. It of course is a lifelong journey, but one that is measured by involvement in the process rather than by achievement.

One approach to discovering our true identity is to find a word that we think describes who we truly are.

Finding our word is sometimes a frustrating process. There are many false starts since we put up so many fronts and don't let people near us to see what the heart of our soul and personality is. However, honest prayer, reflection, speaking with friends, and questioning the guides in our life can help the journey toward finding our true self and in turn, with this sensitivity to the truth about ourselves in hand, to appreciate the presence of God as well.

Once we have a more correct word or name, we can then be freer and more integrated, we can be sensitive to all people in the same way. This will save energy and help us to develop as persons, instead of wasting the energy involved in trying to develop several personalities or faces simultaneously.

In addition, it will help us better monitor the messages we give ourselves all day. That is what is referred to in psychology as self-talk. With a real sense of self we can approach situations with a greater sense of certainty and humility. Consequently, rather than seeking approval or reinforcement, we act out of our identity. If positive results occur, fine; if negative ones occur, well, fine too.

 *Being*

As we listen to our heart and find a sense of identity (our *word*) in which to rest and bring to reflection or prayer, we then can act out of that identity in a true and spontaneous way. Rather than drifting or fighting with life, we can flow with it naturally; this is truly being who we can be in life.

Without a sense of who we are, we wobble with the wrong identity. We take for granted that we know who we are. We make the mistake of never taking the time to listen to, find, and nurture who we are *now*, at this stage of our lives.

Yet, with some courage and reflection, we can discover not only who we are, but revel in the beauty that we find in ourselves so that we can share it freely with others. To do this, however, takes a bit of effort. It likewise requires a quiet little place in our lives where our spirit can breathe deeply, rest, and learn.

~ *Identity* ~

God creates people with inherent value. So, no mistake, failure, loss of image, exaggerated thinking, or hurtful comments by others can take this away or destroy this reality. We must stubbornly hold onto this fact of faith each day, for ourselves, for others, and in gratitude for being made in God's image. Because in "hating the sin, not the sinner" we will be in a position to embrace and learn from criticism without being crushed by it or hating the critic. And, in working hard at adopting this psychologically healthy way of thinking we will be making an important spiritual statement of faith to ourselves and the world each day: "My identity and value come from being a creation of God…and from nowhere else!"

~ *A Simple, Powerful Gift* ~

It would be good for us to remember that one of the greatest gifts we can share with others in pain, despair, or confusion is a clear sense of our own peace and knowledge that we are loved.

Already of Value

Jesus knew he was loved. *He didn't give to others in order to be loved; he gave because he was in love.* One of the most dramatic steps you can take in becoming a person who is more generous with others is to learn to like yourself and to appreciate that you are a special creation of God entirely independent of the world's view. The reality we should model then is: Because of Christ's love we are *already* important.

A Small Dark Chapel

As I enter a small dark chapel
I feel I'm returning home
silently welcomed by Someone
who expected me all along.

Taking a seat in a back row
I settle for a time
to enjoy the glow of candles
and rest here for awhile.

The incense of an earlier hour
still lingers in a haze
with a scent so softly present
there's mystery in the air.

Then in my mind's eye
I clearly begin to see
the joys and tears of others
who prayed before me here.

They sat on wooden benches
and shared their doubt and pain
thankful they could come in need
to find peace once again.

And as I leave I'm grateful
that I've come here as well
to find silence and some healing
in a small dark chapel...God calls home.

IV

Ordinariness

Relationships
Love and Service
Living in the "Now"

Evening Prayer

Now, as I watch the fading soft colors of dusk,
I pause, breathe deeply, and remember You.
My heart is tired, yet I am filled with hope.
My body aches, but my spirit is at home.

As I stretch and lie down for the evening,
Let my worrying cease,
my tired muscles relax,
my nose stop running,
my plans wait for morning…
My heart be at peace.

Yes, let me sleep in Your arms
Until a fresh clear morning awakens me,
So I can greet You with love…once again.

Amen.

~ *Spiritual Guides* ~

We need a spirituality—an openness to a wonderful relationship with the truth about ourselves, others, and God—that is not just a vague urge to feel more at peace. We need an attitude of single-heartedness that is joined with a real sense of identity that is not based on others' views, but on a deep belief in our own unique value. When we have single-heartedness, identity, and compassion as our guides, then an attitude of greater simplicity and continued spiritual progress become possible. We can be in a spiritual and psychological place in which we appreciate our "ordinary" self rather than being overcome by our previously scattered nature or the fantasy that we need to do something spectacular to overcome our sense of stagnation.

We will have direction, and our quiet time will be like the lights of a car that shine upon where we need to move next in the darkness. We will simply put one foot in front of the other, knowing that we are not drifting or being driven, but are actually flowing with life...a gentle, passionate life marked by deep joy.

~ *A Gift of Freedom* ~

An attitude of ordinariness, which is a key source of simplicity, is a gift of freedom not only to ourselves but also to others who encounter us when we are in this open, gentle place. I guess that this shouldn't be too surprising to us, though. For isn't it true that any real grace that we embrace fully for ourselves is one that naturally winds up being shared with others, almost without our even having to think about it?

~ *Honest Friendship* ~

If we really do wish to live deeply spiritual lives ourselves and to help others live this way in today's confusing times, there is no alternative to expending the necessary energy required in being a sensitive friend to others in need.

We must learn to face one another in understanding and love. However, to do this we also must be realistic and have the humility to pray each day for patience, wisdom, charity, and forgiveness—not only of other's failings but of our own as well. Otherwise we will quickly become disillusioned by our own shortcomings and the limitations of others when our day-to-day interactions don't reflect the hopes we had for them.

True intimacy can cause confusion as often as clarity; it produces disagreement along with harmony; it results in exhaustion sometimes well equal to the exhilaration we may experience. The simple truth, which all of us know, is that sharing and receiving love in concrete ways is often painful.

However, despite the true pain of intimacy, it is in honest friendship that we really learn about ourselves. It is in real relationship that (although our own-fashioned images are sometimes bruised) our God-given ordinariness is continually rediscovered in some profound way.

Questions on Our Circle of Friends

Do I have people with whom I can simply be myself?
What type of friends do I value most? Why?
What do I feel are the main qualities of friendship?

List and briefly describe the friends who are now in my life.

Describe ones who are no longer alive or present to me now but who have made an impact on my life. Why do I think they made such a difference in my life?

Among my circle of friends, who are my personal heroes or role models?

Who are the prophets in my life? In other words, who confronts me with the question: To what voices am I responding in life?

Who helps me see my relationships, mission in life, and self-image more clearly? How do they accomplish this?

Who encourages me in a genuine way through praise and a nurturing spirit?

Who teases me into gaining a new perspective when I am too preoccupied or tied up in myself?

Who helps me experience the living God in new ways and helps me let go of stagnant images of the Lord as well as outmoded ways of praying?

～ *Reaching Out...Reaching In* ～

We need to see what we can do for others in life if we are to have joy within us. For it is in living lives open to others that we find our own true selves.

~ Ordinary Life ~

Sensitivity to the presence of God in self and others and during those precious moments of prayerful stillness is not a nicety. It is:

- a graced appreciation of the fact that what is real and ordinary is a sanctuary for the sacred, a chance to meet God;

- a special chance to embrace the spiritual self-esteem that can only come from being gratefully aware of the unique divine presence in us;

- an invitation to go forward with others and compassionately build a world that is truly a gentle place for all of us to grow together before God.

And isn't this what ordinary life, the truly spiritual life, is supposed to be all about?

~ The Essence of Friendship ~

Too often we fail in relationships because we are not willing to accept the wonderful yet limited gifts we have to offer others. Instead, we often feel we are "not enough" as persons. We believe we must be able to do the spectacular or otherwise risk rejection.

And so, frequently we get frustrated when our effort to be amazing by trying to meet everyone's needs, no matter how great they are, fails.

Although dramatic actions are sometimes necessary, they are not the essence of friendship. Nor are they the sign of our being worthwhile, caring members of the community we call "the people of God." A simple sharing of self is.

~ *Love Your Neighbor as Yourself* ~

To have healthy relationships with others we must be clear about our relationship with ourselves. Our relationship with self determines how we will deal with the world. If we lack confidence, we may well interpret the actions and motivations of others inappropriately in a negative way and react with unnecessary fear, anger, or distress. If we can appreciate the presence of God in ourselves as we have been created, we will be more open to finding God in others *as they are*. Consequently, we will not have predetermined expectations of others' behavior—even if they are very different, "alien," or even "the enemy." Then we will love our neighbors as ourselves; we will be in solidarity with others as a unique people who are among the people of God.

~ *Remember to Say...* ~

When you have made a mistake, remember to say to yourself: "Of course I have made a mistake. When you care you will make mistakes. The more you reach out, the more mistakes you make. As a matter of fact if you are not making mistakes now and then, you are probably living too narrowly and diffidently because of an inordinate fear of what people will think if you fail."

When people are angry at you, remember to say to yourself: "It is good that people feel they can be angry at me and don't have to worry that I will overreact in return. Just because they are angry at me doesn't make me a bad person or mean that their anger is capable of destroying me. It gives me a chance to practice poise in such situations and to assertively stand up for what I believe as a way to practice and model it for others."

If you don't succeed, remember to say to yourself: "I can't reach everyone. I can try to be of help to different kinds of people, but it is dangerous for me to believe I am God or to accept the expectations some people put on me to have all the answers or to be able to meet all their demands in the way they want and when they want."

When you feel like a hypocrite, in suggesting steps to others on how to overcome resistances to growth and change that you don't take yourself, remember to say to yourself: "Let me try to 'practice more often what I preach,' so I can make this a more collaborative journey. I can practice more and more how to enter the 'promised land' of clarity, generosity, discipline, faithfulness, and love by following the tenets I propose."

When you feel embarrassed, remember to say to yourself: "In a few weeks, months, or years, what will all of this mean in terms of my life and salvation?"

If you are about to have an outburst of anger, remember to say to yourself: "Why am I giving away the power? Let me hold back for a few minutes, hours, or days until I am clear enough to see if this is really important."

When people don't listen, don't appreciate what you do, or make fun of you, remember to say to yourself: "Well, you can't win them all, can you?"

When someone is indirectly hostile or passive-aggressive (by procrastinating, etc.), remember to say to yourself: "Ah, he doesn't know he is behaving like this but all the same I have to be careful he doesn't get to me and in the process waste too much of my energy."

～ Mitzvah ～

Loving is easy if we are in touch with our own humanness and love ourselves. Too often service is an outgrowth of guilt. Yet, guilt is not meant to be a sustaining force. Love is.

Guilt pushes us to do something because it is the right thing to do. Love encourages us to do something because it is the natural thing to do.

Love enables service to be a natural, almost unconscious aspect of living. Compassionate behavior is not ruled by the expectations of ourselves and others. Getting tied into expectations is often the beginning of the end of true service. When we feel we have done a good job or someone else rewards us for meeting his or her expectations, it obviously feels good. However, there must be a wariness about seeking to please so as to be rewarded.

Instead, the focus should be to love simply because loving is what we are called to do by God. We should give with a sense of *mitzvah* (giving and expecting nothing in return). By doing this we are setting the stage for God to act amidst our faith and the faith of the person(s) to whom we are being present.

~ *Simple Compassion* ~

Too often in our search to do something dramatic we miss the opportunity to do something important because the act doesn't seem worthy enough. We are unable to see the symbolic greatness of the small, caring presence we can be in a world seemingly overwhelmed by troubles and stress.

Not Knowing...
Just Appreciating

The spiritual life is not so much filling oneself with love or special reinforcing positive experiences, but allowing the love we already have to blossom. With such an attitude inconsequential concerns lose their power and the possibilities of God can surface. The simple and peaceful life can offer rich encounters with the ultimate if we don't prejudge how God will be made manifest to us. Not knowing how God will appear *in us* and *before us*, we must move ahead with what seems good and look everywhere to see what good may be happening right in front of us.

The Question

God really has only one expectation of us: to *love*. But since we find this (in our lack of hope, trust, and patience) too difficult to accept, we try to break down this call and replace it with our own human-fashioned ones. So, the expectation to love is erased from our hearts, and the expectations to do, achieve, gain acceptance, control, be secure, or look good are put in our heads instead. There they remain as lies to preoccupy and confuse us. The purpose they serve is to help us avoid facing the challenge of the real, the deep, the ultimate, the first and final question of life. However, despite this "advantage" or secondary gain, they still leave us lost until eventually we are willing in humility to embrace the only God-given question we must answer: *"How can I love?"*

⌒ *The Edge of Mystery* ⌒

Even in impasse we can hope, and even in defeat of our best efforts we can be enthusiastic, if only we don't shy away from the only really God-given question we must face in an anxious world: How can I truly love God, myself, and others *now*?

We must recognize that the answer to this question may be good only for the moment. The Spirit moves where she will. Finding out how I must love *now* is the thrill of life; and settling now for the answer I came up with in my response to God yesterday is to try to be secure in a way that will always leave me with the queasy feeling: "I'm missing something." There is never a substitute for searching actively and continually looking in wonder and awe for perspective. We must be willing and patient, in spite of our talents and the call to develop them, to be dependent on the Divine. Being on the edge of mystery with God is what life is all about. And if we don't panic when this mystery seems too much, the light will dawn. After all, this is what Jesus promised, didn't he?

~ *Seamless Spirituality* ~

With love we begin to see our entire day, and the whole array of interactions that are possible, as *opportunity*. No longer is service to God compartmentalized, nor need it be sharply visible. Instead, it is all service, all love, all a time for a form of community life. Yet, for this to be possible, we must become alert to the love hidden in our hearts and in our day through the presence of constant *prayer*.

~ *Faith, Hope, and Love* ~

If our reflective periods are steeped in faith and our imagery is marked by hope, then our behavior can be inspired by love, so that what we do is able to be of true service to God. The opportunities are certainly there. As Martin Buber once said, "All real living is meeting."

Love breaks through all preconceptions we have about what service to others and God actually is. Many of us have a sense of the dramatic and feel that real service can only be appreciated under such circumstances. The truth is obviously that real service need not always be obvious.

⁓ *An Asceticism of Time* ⁓

Being active for Christ is good. Being overwhelmed and too busy, because we don't have an asceticism of time and effort or an attitude that is fired by love instead of being driven by compulsiveness, obviously isn't. We not only have the responsibility to redeem our time, we have the ability to do it if we are willing to let go of our martyr image, set limits for others (given a willingness to recognize and accept our own limits), and be present to the moments of time and people that may be before us now. The choice is really not someone else's—despite our claim that our schedule is too full or others ask too much of us. The choice is actually ours—and we are asked to prayerfully make it each day. Ironically, not to prayerfully make such choices each day may well be more of an evasion of grace than not doing enough.

~ *Living in the Present* ~

Be sensitive to the moment in which we are now by having a true awareness of the reality of the limited time we have at our disposal.

The present moment is something very precious. It is a fleeting moment of grace we need to value, for there will never be another one like it. The problem is that we often don't appreciate the *now* while it is before us. We think about it only later, when the true energy of being in the moment is gone. Thus, to appreciate the *now* we must take responsibility for attending to it and acknowledging our role in the loss of the experience if we do not achieve full awareness.

Slowing Down the ~ *Frames of Life* ~

It is very easy to fall into the rhythm of a life of business, worry, complaints, hurrying, ignoring, and resentment. The tempo of the sensitive life is something different. It is one in which we pay attention; we are alert to what is happening and really take note of the people and life around us. Sensitive people slow down the frames of life because they value the process rather than the products of interactions. If only more of us were like that.

～ *Stopping to Breathe* ～

Reflections during the day help us to be more present to what is happening to us in the "now." Someone once said that "Life is something that happens to us while we are busy doing something else." A reflective attitude toward life helps us to not be lost in our musings or asleep to the possibilities in life. Furthermore, it is not hard to do.

It only takes a few seconds to stop, breathe, and image yourself with God. As well as during work, it can be done in the car, when walking from one place to another, or waiting on a line in the bank. I also encourage people to image themselves as they believe God truly created them and reflect on how they are acting and interacting during the day based on this image.

～ *Ordinariness* ～

The spirit of ordinariness invites each of us to follow the will of God by trying to find out what our inner motivations and talents are and then to express them without reserve or self-consciousness. This is true ordinariness. Although the call to be ordinary may be simple, it is not easy! And, because very few of us appreciate this subtle, yet profound, distinction, "being ordinary" is extraordinary, even in our times. There is little call in the world today to "just be yourself." Only a few persons are graced with the freedom to recognize the waste and illusion of trying to be someone other than who they are called to be.

~ *Don't Miss It* ~

The *now* is a simple gift that either we are there to receive or we are not. Excuses, no matter how good, unfortunately can't change that. In our lives we have only so much time to appreciate what is before us. If we miss it, so be it.

Too often the reason we do miss the wonder of the *now* is that we are preoccupied with the past or the future. Maybe what would help us avoid spending our time inside the silver casket of nostalgia or continually preoccupied with what lies ahead would be a simple, stark awareness of our own limitedness, our impending death some time in the future.

~ *The Importance of "Now"* ~

With perspective and gratitude, we are surrounded with gifts; we value "the now" so much because we don't know if tomorrow will come. When we have such an attitude, we find that what is already there before us which is good becomes more visible.

Being in *the now* is very much tied to Jesus' phrase: "To whom much has been given, more will be added." The spiritual reality again: "If your eye is good, your whole body will be good" (Mt 6:22). Perceiving *the now* as a gift can make all the difference in how we enjoy the present.

Being in *the now* is not merely paying attention during a peak experience. It is being aware in all settings, seeing the real food of what is to be learned and experienced—not the imaginary, menu food of a future fantasy.

~ *Remember* ~

Are we in touch with God in our depths? Are we single-hearted enough? Are we remembering the single, dramatic call of Christ to remember? To remember what? To remember to *love*—to love strongly, to love always, to love the unlovable within ourselves, as well as the unlovable among those we meet and those we hear and read about (our distant "family").

Moments of alienation and depression can help us to raise our eyes to view a new horizon of hope instead of a darkness of spirit. They can awaken us to embrace our inner fragmentation and our outer interpersonal fences. They can shake us out of our complacency and righteousness and, in a gentle spirit, open us up to God.

And so, next time we feel low, maybe it is not a time to cry or run. Maybe it is a time to sit or kneel and wrap ourselves in gratitude to God. Gratitude for everything is needed—including the very act of stopping us or slowing us down so we can see how we have forgotten to love the presence of God in all creatures, including ourselves.

∼ *Trust and Doubt* ∼

Persons of faith, at some level, are ready for crises, in the same way that they are ready for *all* daily occurrences, to open up new doors.

So, although a crisis is just as painful for the spiritual person as it is for one who has little or no conscious faith, in the faith-full individual the doubt does not point only to despair but—amidst the pain—to new hopes built on a renewed faith and a new dynamic image of God. As a matter of fact, the amount of real trust we have in God is sometimes best measured by the depth of the doubt and the seriousness of the questions with which we are willing to live.

Rather than removing the doubts, prayer may instead help us more and more to see the truth and hold onto the possible as well as the probable without pain. Serious believers are critical thinkers. When a crisis dawns and threatens the very core of their identity and their faith, they are willing to continue to respond and search because of their belief in the *living* God and a desire to live with that God now in some new way, rather than to merely exist.

The Elusiveness of God

When God doesn't answer us as we would like, we feel unfairly tested. We are furious and doubtful about God's presence in our lives. We are angry about what we perceive as the hide-and-seek game God is playing with us at a time when we feel that the divine presence is dramatically needed. If we are really being honest with ourselves, at times like these we may question whether a God exists at all.

When a serious crisis arises, we argue, bargain, express our feelings of abandonment, and become angry or hurt that God is allowing this to happen. We believe this to be "malevolent neglect." In response, it is no wonder that we become *noisy*. Now this style of relating to God and God's messages to us is actually not really bad.

Expressing anguish, disillusionment, and near despair with a deeply felt desire for a return of what we have lost or to a pre-crisis state is natural. As a matter of fact, it may be one of the signs of a faith that is real and based on an ongoing relationship with the living God.

~ *Nourishment* ~

Good yearnings bring us to the edge of a new spiritual field filled with the riches of potentially rewarding relationships with old tattered books, new ideas, and an intricate tapestry of friends—some known, some unique, some challenging, all good.

We need to be open to what is right before us and enjoy new worlds of books, museums, relationships, and experiences with nature. We need to start to let these forms of nourishment fill us with joy and perspective.

There is so much there for us if we look. As a matter of fact, once we start realizing what nourishment is actually available, rather than spiritual boredom, we will have to decide instead the answer to the question: What should I enjoy or experience *next*?

The Lord's comment to his disciples that to those who have been given much, more will be given is borne out when we get involved in activities and experiences that are truly renewing....Such food for our soul not only feeds us now but also opens up new possibilities that we might not have even considered. The wonderful possibilities are endless.

～ The "Fruits" ～

We often need someone to give us the permission to do what is reasonable: to move away from the list of rules that we have set up for ourselves so that we can explore other ways of living our lives. Not only can therapy and spiritual guidance help in this regard, but so can speaking with our friends and even thinking things through ourselves. The simple dictum, "What are the fruits?" will help us. If the fruits of our rules are anxiety and stress, we have to ask if the rules that we have made up are really good ones. Likewise, we have to be careful that the rules we have made don't become somehow spiritualized into rules that *God* has given us. We just don't know that much to make such overarching rules. We need help for such guiding principles, and that is why a community of friends and a philosophy of living that is open to new information and change are necessary; with their help, we can greet each different phase of life in a healthier way.

— *A Contemplative Attitude* —

We need to develop a *contemplative attitude toward life in general* if we are to nurture and sustain a rich healthy inner life.

Several ways we can do this are by:

- *listening* (a very important word) to the people and the world around us, because it is in and through people and events that we encounter God and what God is calling us to be;

- *prioritizing* the God-relationship in our lives by recognizing the importance of both personal and communal prayer and then acting accordingly;

- *reading and praying with scripture*, where we encounter God's self-revelation most directly;

- *maintaining a healthy balance* between structure and freedom; action and contemplation; personal and communal prayer/worship;

- making efforts to nurture our faith through *spiritual reading, good conversation, and ongoing education;*

106

- *opening ourselves* (despite the pain that may be associated with it) to the possibilities of grace that fill and surround us and sometimes the kinds of grace that even come kicking, scratching, or begging at our door.

~ *Graced Self-Awareness* ~

Grace is to be recognized and greeted with all of the energy, knowledge, and willingness we can muster. Otherwise it will be missed, taken for granted, or willfully ignored due to our narcissism or anxiety. Burying our talents in these difficult, needy times is a subtle form of sinfulness that no one can afford. To do so is not only foolish, but also dangerous—for ourselves and the needy world in which we live.

However, discernment, true self-awareness, appreciating our personal theology, and theological reflection are *spiritual* movements—this point can't be emphasized enough. Without grace, without God, there is no true process of sensitively discerning who we are and who we are called to be.

~ *Hope* ~

When one is suffering one must remember the important reality of hope. Hope isn't simply believing that things will go well because one is a good person who deserves such rewards. Instead, hope is an attitude of living that makes one seek and find new possibilities because of an attitude of trust.

~ *Deep Gratefulness* ~

For most of us, deep gratefulness—a natural sense of appreciation for breath, food, friends, good music, books, long leisurely walks, and other gifts of life—must be cultivated. Our demanding society goes against this trend. Its messages are as follows: "You don't have enough!" "Be careful that you're not being cheated in some way of what you deserve!"

Yet, when we learn to taste gratitude and we can enjoy living fully with awe, our eyes will be opened to a new reality that will fill the part of our heart that feels so empty now. No matter how ungrateful and demanding we may feel at times, what more can we ask than this?

~ *Prophetic Guidance* ~

What if, in the spirit of ammas and abbas of the African desert, we were able to begin each day afresh without worry or agendas? What would we do as an encore? If we didn't fill our hearts and heads with worry, the desire to control, or addictions, but "simply" enjoyed what was before us and found God there, what would we have to complain about most of the time? How would we live an undistracted life that would force us to then face the angst of our own limitedness, helplessness, lies, and our own eventual death? These are the questions with which prophets help us.

Prophets point! They point to the fact that it doesn't matter whether pleasure or pain is involved; the only thing that matters is that we seek to be with God in what we do and how we think, feel, and image ourselves and the world. In other words, we seek to see and live "the truth" because only it will set us free.

Nurturing a Hopeful Heart

Read a bit

Listen to a favorite song

Call a friend

Remember a kindness

Help the poor

Keep perspective

Smile broadly

Laugh loudly

Close doors gently

Do what you can

Live gratefully

Relax for a moment

Breathe deeply

Tease yourself often

Take a quiet walk...

Tell God a funny story

Come Sit by Me

When I am tired God says,
"Come sit by me."

I speak about the little
things that have happened to me
during the day
and I am heard.

I share my fears,
angers, doubts,
and sorrows,
and I am held.

I smile with what energy
I have left
and I am gently teased.

Then when all the conversation
is over and the day has been opened up
and emptied out,
I am ready for rest.

Nothing is solved.
Nothing is under control.
But also nothing pressing remains.

But as I go to sleep a fleeting thought
breaks the smooth surface of my peace:

What would I do each night
if God didn't say:
"Come sit by me"?

Key to Sources

Books by Robert J. Wicks used in this collection:

Af   *After 50: Spiritually Embracing Your Own Wisdom Years*. Mahwah, N.J.: Paulist Press, 1997.

Lg   *Living a Gentle, Passionate Life*. Mahwah, N.J.: Paulist Press, 1998.

Ls   *Living Simply in an Anxious World*. Mahwah, N.J.: Paulist Press, 1998.

NPP   *Not previously published*

Ss   *Seeds of Sensitivity: Deepening Your Spiritual Life*. Notre Dame, Ind.: Ave Maria Press, 1995.

Sp   *Seeking Perspective: Weaving Spirituality and Psychology in Search of Clarity*. Mahwah, N.J.: Paulist Press, 1991 (out of print).

T   *Touching the Holy: Ordinariness, Self-Esteem, and Friendship*. Notre Dame, Ind.: Ave Maria Press, 1992.

Guide to Quote Sources

Snow Falling on Snow . . . NPP

I. Experiencing the Lord

II. Availability

III. Clarity

117

IV. Ordinariness